The Ladybird Key Words Reading Scheme is based on these commonly used words. Those used most often in the English language are introduced first—with othappeal to children. All th covered in the early books use further word lists to fluency. The total numbe which will be learned in the complete reading scheme is nearly two thousand. The gradual introduction of these words, frequent repetition and complete 'carry-over' from book to book, will ensure rapid learning.

The full-colour illustrations have been designed to create a desirable attitude towards learning—by making every child *eager* to read each title. Thus this attractive reading scheme embraces not only the latest findings in word frequency, but also the natural interests and activities of happy children.

Each book contains a list of the new words introduced.

W. MURRAY, the author of the Ladybird Key Words Reading Scheme, is an experienced headmaster, author and lecturer on the teaching of reading. He is co-author, with J. McNally, of 'Key Words to Literacy'—a teacher's book published by The Schoolmaster Publishing Co. Ltd.

THE LADYBIRD KEY WORDS READING SCHEME has 12 graded books in each of its three series—**'a'**, **'b'** and **'c'**. As explained in the handbook 'Teaching Reading', these 36 graded books are all written on a controlled vocabulary, and take the learner from the earliest stages of reading to reading fluency.

The **'a'** series gradually introduces and repeats new words. The parallel **'b'** series gives the needed further repetition of these words at each stage, but in different context and with different illustrations.

The **'c'** series is also parallel to the **'a'** series, and supplies the necessary link with writing and phonic training.

An illustrated booklet—'Notes for Teachers'—can be obtained free from the publishers. This booklet fully explains the Key Words principle and the Ladybird Key Words Reading Scheme. It also includes information on the reading books, work books and apparatus available, and such details as the vocabulary loading and reading ages of all books.

BOOK 6c
The Ladybird Key Words Reading Scheme

Reading with sounds

by W. MURRAY
with illustrations
by MARTIN AITCHISON

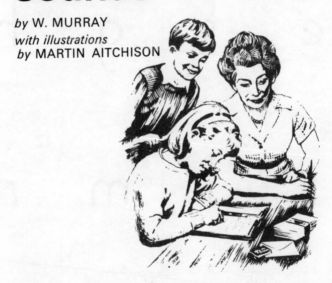

Publishers: Ladybird Books Ltd . Loughborough
© Ladybird Books Ltd (formerly Wills & Hepworth Ltd) 1965,
Printed in England

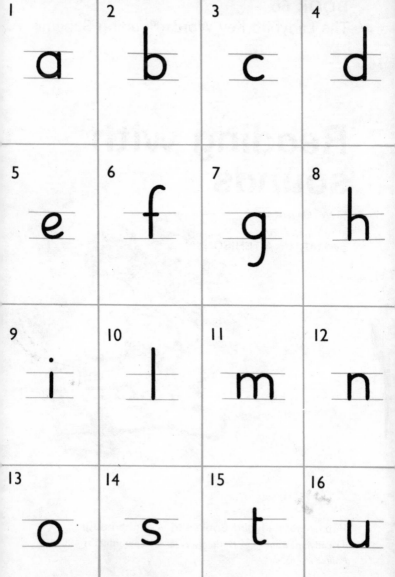

1 a	2 b	3 c	4 d
5 e	6 f	7 g	8 h
9 i	10 l	11 m	12 n
13 o	14 s	15 t	16 u

Sounds we know from Books 4c and 5c

Here is a pig.

p Say the word **pig**.

What is the sound
    when you start to say **pig**?

Here is a pen.

p Say the word **pen**.

You make the **p** sound
    when you start to say **pen**.

Here is a pencil.

p Say the word **pencil**.

What is the sound
    when you start to say **pencil**?

Here is a picture.

p Say the word **picture**.

You make the **p** sound
    when you start to say **picture**.

p

p

p

p

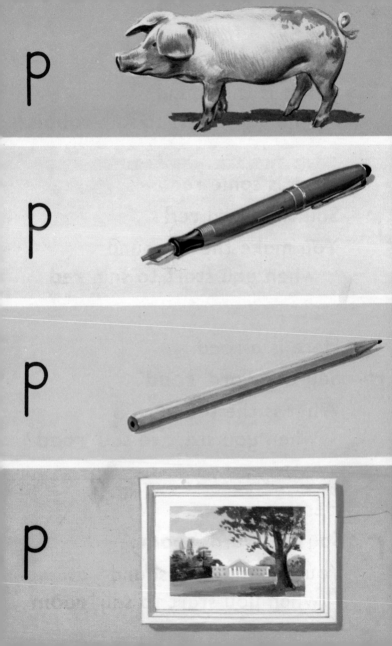

Here is a rabbit.

r Say the word **rabbit**.

What is the sound
when you start to say **rabbit**?

Here is some red.

r Say the word **red**.

You make the **r** sound
when you start to say **red**.

Here is a road.

r Say the word **road**.

What is the sound
when you start to say **road**?

Here is a room.

r Say the word **room**.

You make the **r** sound
when you start to say **room**.

r

r

r

r

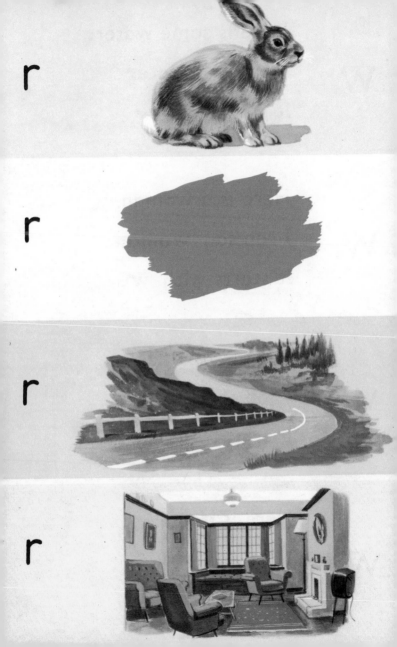

Here is some water.

W

I can say **water**.

It starts with **w**.

Here is a woman.

W

I can say **woman**.

It starts with **w**.

Here is a window.

W

I can say **window**.

It starts with **w**.

Here is a wall.

W

I can say **wall**.

It starts with **w**.

W

W

W

W

j

This is some jam.

You can say **jam** .

It starts with **j** .

j

This is some jelly.

You can say **jelly** .

It starts with **j** .

j

This is a jug.

You can say **jug** .

It starts with **j** .

j

This is a jar.

You can say **jar** .

It starts with **j** .

j

j

j

j

Complete the words as you write them
in your exercise book.
The pictures will help you.

p r w j

1 –ot

2 –ug

3 –et

4 –ar

5 –ag

6 –am

7 –all

8 –eg

The answers are on Page 48

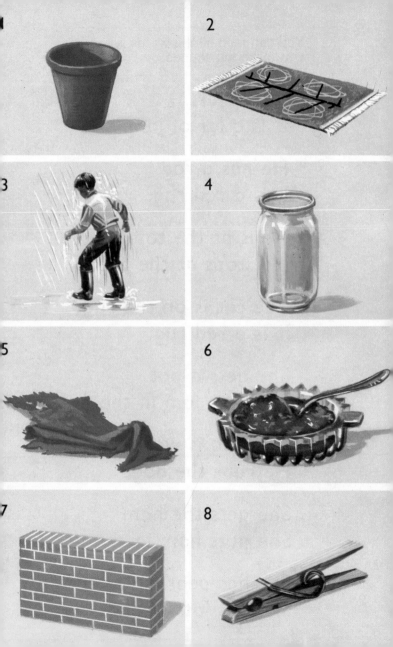

You can read all the words when
you make the sounds.

1. It is a jar.
   It is a jar of jam.

2. He has a rag.
   It is a red rag.

3. He is at the top.
   He stops at the top.

4. The cat is on the rug.
   It is a red rug.

5. She gets a pot.
   She puts jam in the pot.

6. The dog is wet.
   He rubs the dog.

7. She gets the ham.
   She puts ham in the pan.

8. She has pegs.
   She has lots of pegs.

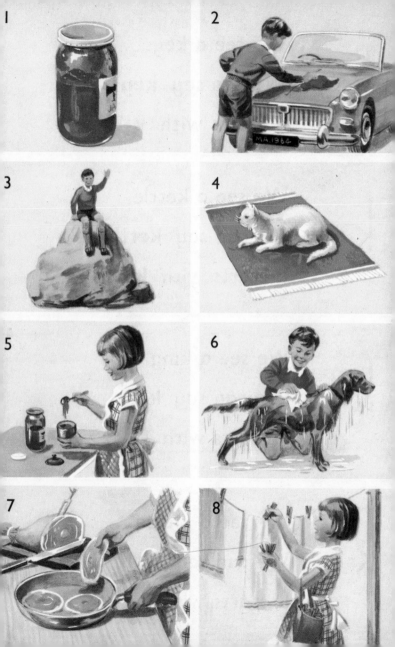

1

2

3

4

5

6

7

8

k

We see a key.

We can say **key**.

It starts with **k**.

---

k

We see a kettle.

We can say **kettle**.

It starts with **k**.

---

k

We see a king.

We can say **king**.

It starts with **k**.

---

k

We see a kitten.

We can say **kitten**.

It starts with **k**.

k

k

k

k

Look at the van.

V   You say **van**.

It starts with **v**.

Look at the vase.

V   You say **vase**.

It starts with **v**.

Look at the vine.

V   You say **vine**.

It starts with **v**.

Look at the violin.

V   You say **violin**.

It starts with **v**.

V

V

V

V

x as in **box**.

X

x as in **fox**.

---

y

y for **yellow**.

---

z for **zebra**.

and

z for **zoo**.

x

y

z

Complete the words as you write them
in your exercise book.
The pictures will help you.

a e i o u

1 p–g

2 t–n

3 c–t

4 c–r

5 p–g

6 p–n

7 r–g

8 m–g

9 t–p

10 p–t

The answers are on Page 48

qu for **quarter**.

Here is a quarter.

qu for **queen**.

Here is a queen.

qu for **quill**.

Here is a quill.

qu

qu

qu

Grandfather and Grandmother write to say that they want to go away to the sea. They want Dad and the children to look after their dog, their house and their garden when they are away.

Mum reads the letter to Peter and Jane.

Jane says, " Good. I want to look after the house." Peter says, " Yes, it will be fun. I will take the dog out every day, and we can all look after the garden."

" Let us write a letter to Grandmother and Grandfather," says Jane.

" Yes," says Peter. " We will do it now."

Copy out and complete—

1. Mum reads to —eter and Jane.

2. Grandfather and Grandmother —ant to go away.

3. Peter and —ane will help.

4. Peter says, " —es, I want to do it."

The answers are on Page 48

The children write to their Grandmother and Grandfather.

Jane has a pencil and she writes down the words. Mum and Peter help her. They tell Jane what to write. Jane writes—

Dear Grandmother and Grandfather,

Thank you for your letter. We will look after your house and garden when you are at the sea. We like to help you very much.

We will take the dog out every day for a walk and we will look after the birds and flowers.

Have a good time at the sea.

Love from,

Jane and Peter.

Copy out and complete—

1. They —ant —o write.

2. Jane —as a —encil.

3. They like to help —ery much.

4. We w—ll take the d—g out.

The answers are on Page 49

Dear
Grandmother
and
Grandfather,
Thank you
for

Peter's father takes his own father and mother to the station by car. Peter and Jane are with them. The children are going to see their Grandmother and Grandfather off.

At the station Peter and his sister help Grandmother and Grandfather out of the car. Dad has the bags.

They find the train in the station. Soon Grandfather and Grandmother are in the train.

"Look after each other," says Dad.

"Yes, we will," says Grandfather.

"Have a good time," say the children.

Then the train pulls out of the station.

Copy out and complete—

1. Peter's —ather has a car.
2. Dad has the —ags.
3. Peter and Jane look —p at the train.
4. The children are —ot in the train.

The answers are on Page 49

Here are Dad, Peter and Jane at Grandfather's house. They have come by car. Jane has her baby doll Ann with her today.

They go into the house. They have been here lots of times before. The children like to come to this house. They love their Grandfather and their Grandmother very much.

Soon they start to work. Jane does the work in the house and Peter and his father go into the garden.

Peter looks for Grandfather's dog. He wants to take him for a walk.

Copy out and complete—

1. They are —t their Grandfather's
                                    house.
2. They —o into the house.
3. —oon they start to work.
4. Peter —ooks for the —og.

The answers are on Page 49

Peter is out with the dog. He takes him where he can run about.

It is a very hot day. Peter finds it best to walk under the trees because it is not so hot there. The trees are by the water.

Peter sits on a wall by the water. He looks at some other boys as they play with a ball. One of the boys lets the ball go into the water.

Peter tells the dog to go into the water. The dog jumps in and gets the ball for the boys.

Copy out and complete—

1. The —og likes to —un.
2. The boy l—ts the ball go —nto the water.
3. The dog —an get the —all.
4. He —umps in —or the ball.

The answers are on Page 50

Peter and his father are in Grandfather's garden. Pat is with them.

Jane is with an old friend of her Grandmother who lives next door. This friend is going to let her have some eggs.

Peter's father has work to do. Peter helps him and then he has a game with the dog. The dog likes to jump for a ball and to run after it. It is not so hot now.

There is some water in the garden. Soon Peter lets the ball go into the water. "I will get it," he says.

Copy out and complete—

1. Jane has one, two, three, four, five, si— eggs.
2. The dog —uns and —umps.
3. It is —ot so —ot now.
4. "Loo—," says Peter, "the ball is in the water."

The answers are on Page 50

Jane comes out of the house into the garden. She sees that the ball is in the water and that Peter is going to get it.

"Don't get wet, Peter," she says.

But Peter is soon in the water.

"Help," he says. "Help me, Dad. Help me, Jane. I am in the water. Help me to get out."

Then the dog jumps into the water. He wants to play with Peter.

Dad and Jane run to pull Peter out of the water.

They get him out, but he is very wet.

Copy out and complete—

1. Dad works in the —arden.
2. "Help —e, Jane," says Peter.
3. The dog —ees Peter in the water.
4. Peter is —ery w—t.

The answers are on Page 50

Jane is in the garden. She can see some birds as they fly round the trees. She knows that her Grandmother and Grandfather love birds.

"Grandmother gives them something to eat every day," Jane says. "They look as if they want to eat now. I must get something for them."

She gets some cake and puts it out for the birds. Soon they come down to eat it.

Jane looks at the birds as they eat the cake. Then she gets some flowers from the garden for the friend who lives next door.

Copy out and complete—

1. Jane is —n the garden.
2. She looks at the birds —s they fly round the trees.
3. Jane —ets some cake for the birds.
4. The birds eat the —ake.

The answers are on Page 51

Grandmother and Grandfather have come home today. They have had a good time by the sea.

Here is Grandmother with Jane. She takes off her hat as she sits down to have some tea and to talk to Jane.

Jane tells her about the house, the garden, the dog and the birds. She says that Grandmother's friend next door gave them some eggs.

Then Jane talks about her own friends. She tells Grandmother about Mr and Mrs Green, Bob, Mary and Molly, about Pam, and about old Tom who lives by the sea.

Copy out and complete—

1. Grandmother takes off her h—t.
2. They have —ad a good time.
3. Jane talks about Pa— and B—b.
4. Jane talks about old T—m.

The answers are on Page 51

Grandfather thanks the children for the help they gave when he was away. He says he will take them to the Zoo.

Off they go the next day. Grandfather has no car, so they go by train.

At the Zoo they walk round for some time and then they have something to eat. Then Peter says, "I want to go on the elephant."

Here he is on the elephant. Jane looks at an ostrich. "What a big bird," she says.

The children have a good time at the Zoo, and then they go home. They thank Grandfather very much.

Copy out and complete—

1. Peter and Jane go to the —oo.
2. The children —ike the —oo.
3. Peter gets —p on the —lephant.
4. They thank Grandfather —ery —uch.

The answers are on Page 51

Pages 48 to 51 give the answers to the written exercises in this book.

Page 14

1	pot	2	rug
3	wet	4	jar
5	rag	6	jam
7	wall	8	peg

Page 24

1	pig	2	tin
3	cat	4	car
5	peg	6	pen
7	rug	8	mug
9	top	10	pot

Page 28

1 Mum reads to Peter and Jane.

2 Grandfather and Grandmother want to go away.

3 Peter and Jane will help.

4 Peter says, "Yes, I want to do it."

Page 30 1 They want to write.

2 Jane has a pencil.

3 They like to help very much.

4 We will take the dog out.

Page 32 1 Peter's father has a car.

2 Dad has the bags.

3 Peter and Jane look up at the train.

4 The children are not in the train.

Page 34 1 They are at their Grandfather's house.

2 They go into the house.

3 Soon they start to work.

4 Peter looks for the dog.

Page 42 1 Jane is in the garden.

2 She looks at the birds as they fly round the trees.

3 Jane gets some cake for the birds.

4 The birds eat the cake.

Page 44 1 Grandmother takes off her hat.

2 They have had a good time.

3 Jane talks about Pam and Bob.

4 Jane talks about old Tom.

Page 46 1 Peter and Jane go to the Zoo.

2 The children like the Zoo.

3 Peter gets up on the elephant.

4 They thank Grandfather very much.

Now read Book 7a

Words used

This Book 6c provides the link with writing for the words in the Readers 6a and 6b in the Ladybird Key Words Reading Scheme. It also introduces further phonic training.

All the 52 new words in the parallel Readers 6a and 6b are used in this Book 6c, together with the others learned in the earlier books of the Scheme. In addition the following are introduced to assist phonic training.

Key Words: am, box, dear, jam, pen, pencil, queen, road, room, woman, window, van, year.

Other words: fox, jar, jelly, jug, kettle, key, king, kitten, lot, mug, pan, peg, pot, quarter, quill, rag, rub, rug, six, vase, vine, violin, wall, yellow, zebra, Zoo.